THE MLS
WORLD OF
SOCCER

TRAVEL HOME
WITH MLS STARS

By James Buckley, Jr.

Beach Ball Books

Published by Beach Ball Books LLC
Santa Barbara, Calif.
www.beachballbooks.com

Produced by Shoreline Publishing Group LLC
Santa Barbara, California
www.shorelinepublishing.com
President/Editorial Director: James Buckley, Jr.
Designed by Tom Carling, www.carlingdesign.com
Cover soccer ball illustration by Laurent Davoust
Translation assistance by Annie Buckley

All photographs, including cover, courtesy of Getty Images Sport except the following:
Time & Life Pictures: 6 left, 7; Bob Thomas/Popperfoto: 6 center, 6 right.
Soccer ball flag illustrations by Laurent Davous.

ISBN: 978-1-936310-15-9

10 9 8 7 6 5 4 3 2 1   09 10 11 12 13

This book conforms to CPSIA 2008.

Printed by Asia Pacific, China. April, 2011.

CONTENTS

Major League Soccer was born out of the success of the 1994 World Cup, which was played in the United States. That tournament drew millions of fans, filling stadiums around the country. Soccer-lovers were ready to support a U.S. pro league.

In 1996, ten teams started play in the first MLS season. D.C. United, based in the na-tion's capital, won the first MLS Cup as league champion (see the chart below for all the MLS champs). Over the next decade, the league continued to grow, adding teams in new cities. Two more teams joined MLS in 2011: the Vancouver Whitecaps FC and the Portland Timbers. In 2012, a team will call Montreal home, making it three

ALL-TIME MLS CUP CHAMPIONS

2011	
2010	Colorado Rapids
2009	Real Salt Lake
2008	Columbus Crew
2007	Houston Dynamo
2006	Houston Dynamo
2005	Los Angeles Galaxy
2004	D.C. United
2003	San Jose Earthquakes
2002	Los Angeles Galaxy
2001	San Jose Earthquakes
2000	Kansas City Wizards
1999	D.C. United
1998	Chicago Fire
1997	D.C. United
1996	D.C. United

Canadian teams in the league. That will bring the total of MLS teams to an all-time high of 19!

Over the past 15 seasons, some tremendous soccer stars have played for MLS teams. Most players in the league are from the United States and Canada. These players have greatly helped improve their national teams with the skills and success they earned in MLS play.

But MLS is not just North Americans. Soccer is enormously popular around the world. So far, players from nearly 100

countries have played in the league, with players from new countries joining all the time.

In this book, you'll meet some of the best players in MLS today. You'll read about their successes for their MLS teams. But you'll also visit their homelands. Find out what soccer is like in Brazil or Japan or England. You'll find country facts and soccer facts side by side!

Get your soccer cleats (many players call them "boots") tied on . . . pull up your socks . . . put on your game face . . . and let's travel the World of Soccer!

WORLD STARS!

The Galaxy's David Beckham (England) takes on Seattle's Fredy Montero (Colombia). They're just two of the many international players in MLS.

2011 MLS Teams

Eastern Conference
Chicago Fire
Columbus Crew
D.C. United
Houston Dynamo
New England Revolution
New York Red Bulls
Philadelphia Union
Sporting Kansas City
Toronto FC

Western Conference
Chivas USA
Colorado Rapids
FC Dallas
Los Angeles Galaxy
Portland Timbers
Real Salt Lake
San Jose Earthquakes
Seattle Sounders FC
Vancouver Whitecaps FC

THE WORLD OF SOCCER

History

For most of the past century, soccer has been the most popular sport in the world. Soccer was not invented in one day, as basketball was, for instance. Instead, the sport grew out of several types of ball-kicking sports. Some of those ball games were played thousands of years ago! In the 1850s and 1860s, groups of athletes in England drew up the first written rules for soccer (and for rugby). The most famous were created in London in 1863. Though a few things have changed since those early days, much of soccer today would be familiar to the first players.

WORLD CUP

Held every four years, the World Cup is watched by more people than any other sporting event. After two years of games, 32 teams make the World Cup finals. After another month of games, one team ends up on top as the World Cup champion. The first World Cup was held in 1930; the event was cancelled twice during World War II. Here's a list of all the World Cup winners. The first Women's World Cup was held in 1991 and was won by the United States.

World Cup Champions

2010	Spain	**1986**	Argentina	**1958**	Brazil
2006	Italy	**1982**	Italy	**1954**	West Germany
2002	Brazil	**1978**	Argentina	**1950**	Uruguay
1998	France	**1974**	West Germany	**1938**	Italy
1994	Brazil	**1970**	Brazil	**1934**	Italy
1990	West Germany	**1966**	England	**1930**	Uruguay
		1962	Brazil		

Club and Nation

Today, billions of people cheer for their favorite teams. Most fans root for two different teams: a club, or professional, team; and a national team. Pro clubs play in leagues within one nation (see list of top leagues below). Those clubs pay the players (often enormous amounts!) and try to win their league as well as other events.

Some outstanding players also get a chance to play on a national team. There are national teams beginning with under-16s (teenagers). Playing for his or her nation's top national team is the goal of any pro player. Winning the World Cup is the goal for all those national teams.

Whether rooting for a pro team or waving a flag for the national teams, fans around the globe love watching the "beautiful game."

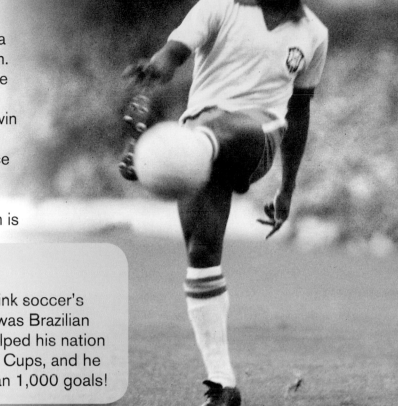

PÉLE!

Many experts think soccer's greatest player was Brazilian star Péle. He helped his nation win three World Cups, and he scored more than 1,000 goals!

TOP LEAGUES

Most countries have some sort of pro league. Some of those leagues stand out for their quality and history. Major League Soccer is the top pro league in the U.S. and Canada. Here are some other important leagues from around the world:

COUNTRY	PRO LEAGUE
England	Premier League
Spain	La Liga
Italy	Serie A (left)
Germany	Bundesliga
Argentina	Primera División
Brazil	Primera Division
Japan	J-League
Mexico	Primera División

FAST FACT
WHY "SOCCER"?

One of the early names for the most popular ball-kicking sport was "association football." In America, with the sport that became NFL football more popular, ball-kicking fans needed a name for their game. The letters "assoc." are short for association, so the name of that game became . . . soccer.

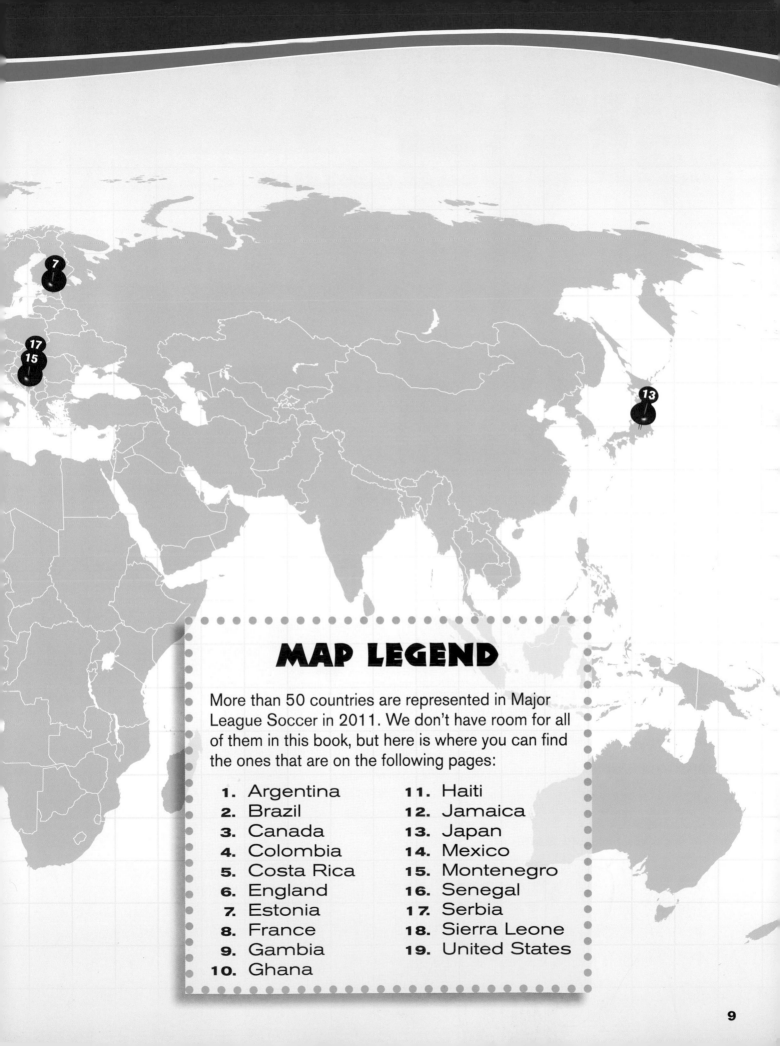

MAP LEGEND

More than 50 countries are represented in Major League Soccer in 2011. We don't have room for all of them in this book, but here is where you can find the ones that are on the following pages:

1. Argentina
2. Brazil
3. Canada
4. Colombia
5. Costa Rica
6. England
7. Estonia
8. France
9. Gambia
10. Ghana
11. Haiti
12. Jamaica
13. Japan
14. Mexico
15. Montenegro
16. Senegal
17. Serbia
18. Sierra Leone
19. United States

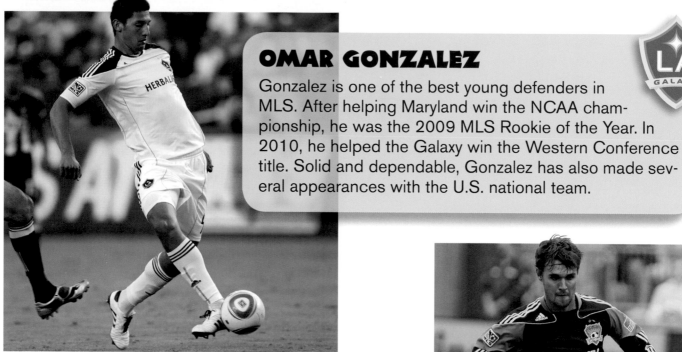

OMAR GONZALEZ

Gonzalez is one of the best young defenders in MLS. After helping Maryland win the NCAA championship, he was the 2009 MLS Rookie of the Year. In 2010, he helped the Galaxy win the Western Conference title. Solid and dependable, Gonzalez has also made several appearances with the U.S. national team.

FACTS ABOUT THE
UNITED STATES

CAPITAL:
Washington DC

POPULATION:
313.3 million

LANGUAGE:
English

WORLD CUP APPEARANCES: 9

WORLD CUP TITLES: 0

▶ The Mississippi is the longest river in the U.S.

▶ Smith is the most common family name in the U.S.

▶ A U.S. win over England in the 1950 World Cup is one of soccer's biggest upsets ever.

▶ America's national bird is the bald eagle.

▶ The highest point? Mt. McKinley in Alaska.

CHRIS WONDOLOWSKI

After a solid but quiet MLS career, Wondolowski burst to the top of the league in 2010. With 18 goals, he led MLS and earned the Golden Boot. In one stretch, the former Houston Dynamo player scored 10 straight goals for San Jose, an all-time MLS record.

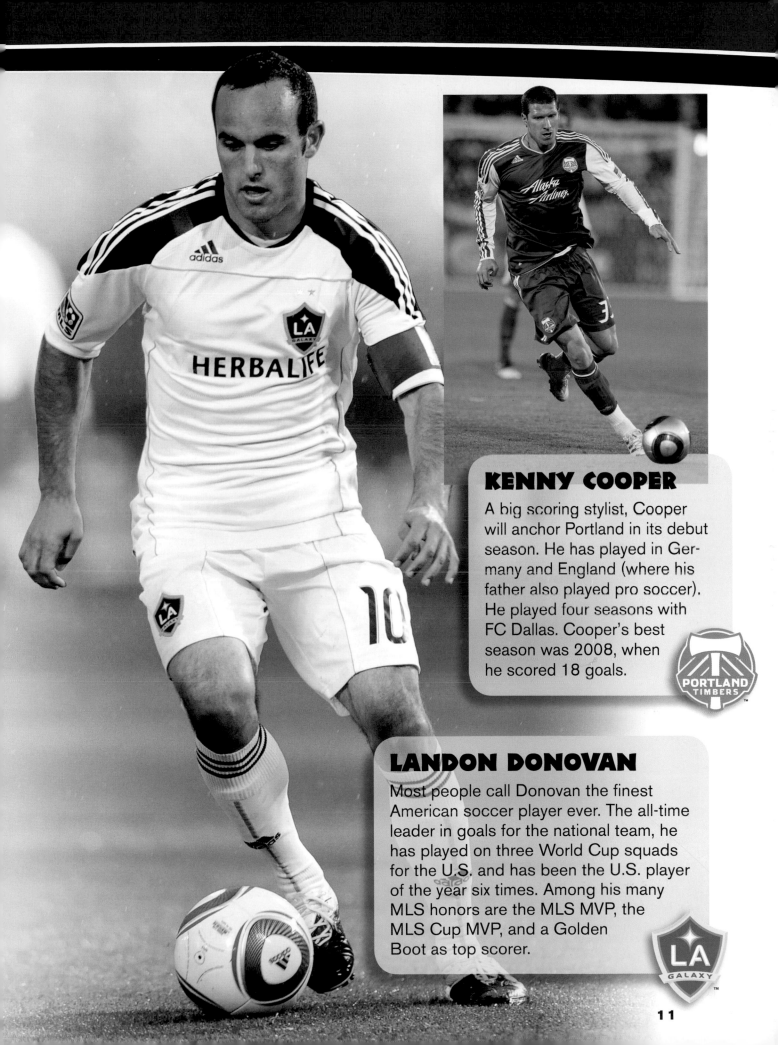

KENNY COOPER

A big scoring stylist, Cooper will anchor Portland in its debut season. He has played in Germany and England (where his father also played pro soccer). He played four seasons with FC Dallas. Cooper's best season was 2008, when he scored 18 goals.

LANDON DONOVAN

Most people call Donovan the finest American soccer player ever. The all-time leader in goals for the national team, he has played on three World Cup squads for the U.S. and has been the U.S. player of the year six times. Among his many MLS honors are the MLS MVP, the MLS Cup MVP, and a Golden Boot as top scorer.

CANADA

TERRY DUNFIELD

Dunfield brings a wealth of international experience to a young Whitecaps team. He grew up in Vancouver but moved to England at 14 to play for Manchester City. He spent 10 years playing for them and various English clubs. He has also played for Canada on many international teams.

SOCCER IN CANADA

Canada's history with soccer goes back to the sport's earliest days. English and Europeans who moved to Canada brought the game with them. Several North American Soccer league teams were in Canada, and the country has had several pro leagues over the years. The latest is the Canadian Soccer League, which is considered a step below MLS. Toronto FC was the first team in MLS outside the United States. A highlight for the men's national team came in 2002, when they won the Gold Cup tournament.

FACTS ABOUT CANADA

CAPITAL: Ottawa

LANGUAGES: English/French

WORLD CUP TITLES: 0

POPULATION: 34 million

WORLD CUP APPEARANCES: 1

MLS PLAYERS 2011: 19

▶ Canada is the second-largest country in the world by area, trailing only Russia.

▶ Parts of far northern Canada reach into the Arctic Circle.

▶ The Canadian dollar has a picture of a bird called a loon, so people call the $1 coin the "loonie."

▶ The Great Bear Rainforest in British Columbia is the northernmost rainforest in the world.

ANDRE HAINAULT

Dynamo fans can count on Hainault to be there no matter what. He has missed only a few minutes of his two seasons as a Houston defensive standout. He played previously in the Czech Republic and in Montreal. He has also helped the national team.

DWAYNE DE ROSARIO

In his 11th season in MLS, De Rosario is the most successful Canadian ever in the league. His 242 games and 62 goals (through 2010) are most among Canadians. After playing for San Jose and Houston, he joined Toronto in 2009 and was the team's MVP with a team-record 15 goals in 2010. He joined the Red Bulls for 2011. His 52 career goals are fourth-most for Canada's national team.

FRANCISCO MENDOZA

A key midfield player, Mendoza has appeared in more MLS games than any other player from Mexico. He rejoined the team in 2011; he first played for Chivas USA from 2005–08.

Un mediocampista importante, Mendoza ha aparecido en más partidos de la MLS que cualquier otro jugador de México. Mendoza jugó por primera vez con Chivas USA en 2005-2008 y se reunió con el equipo en 2011.

SOCCER IN **MEXICO**

The sport is enormously popular in Mexico. The whole country seems to stop when the national team plays. Teams in the professional Primera División draw huge crowds. Chivas de Guadalajara has won the most league titles with 11. Mexico hosted the FIFA World Cup in 1970 and 1986.

Fútbol en México: El deporte es enormemente popular en México. Todo el país parece parar cuando juega la selección nacional. Los equipos en la Primera División atraen a grandes multitudes. Chivas de Guadalajara ha ganado 11 títulos de la liga, más que cualquier otro equipo! México fue la sede de la Copa Mundial de la FIFA en 1970 y 1986.

FACTS ABOUT **MEXICO**

CAPITAL: Mexico City

POPULATION: 107.5 million

LANGUAGE: Spanish

WORLD CUP APPEARANCES: 13

WORLD CUP TITLES: 0

MLS PLAYERS 2011: 9

▶ Mexico celebrates its Independence Day on September 16. On that day in 1810, they declared independence from Spain.

▶ Founded in 1325, Mexico City is the oldest major city in North America.

▶ Mexico is home to ancient ruins—including the famous Chichen Itza temple— of the Mayan people who lived more than 600 years ago.

▶ Thank Mexico next time you eat chocolate—that tasty treat was first created in Mexico by ancient Mayans.

RAFA MARQUEZ

Few players from Mexico have been as successful as Rafa. He helped Barcelona win numerous championships before moving to New York in 2010. He is also the captain of the Mexican National Team, for whom he has played 101 games.

Pocos jugadores de México han tenido tanto exito como Rafa quien ayudó al Barcelona a ganar numerosos campeonatos antes de que se transfiriera a Nueva york en 2010. Tambien es el capitan de la Selección Nacional de México, para quien ha jugado 101 partidos.

OMAR BRAVO

A talented striker, Bravo's experience with Chivas de Guadalajara of the Mexican league and with the Mexican National Team will be a huge help to his new teammates on Sporting KC He was the second-leading scorer in Chivas history!

Un delantero talentoso, las experiencias de Bravo con las Chivas de Guadalajara de la liga Mexicana y con la Selección Mexicana ayudarán inmensamente a sus compañeros de equipo en Sporting KCi Fue el segundo mayor goleador en la historia de Chivas!

COSTA RICA

CAPITAL: San Jose

POPULATION: 4.5 million

LANGUAGE: Spanish

WORLD CUP APPEARANCES: 3   **WORLD CUP TITLES:** 0

MLS PLAYERS 2011: 7

▶ Became independent from Spain in 1838.

▶ Costa Rica gets almost all of its electricity using clean, natural sources.

▶ In 2010, Laura Chinchilla became the first woman president of Costa Rica.

▶ A nickname for people from Costa Rica is "Ticos."

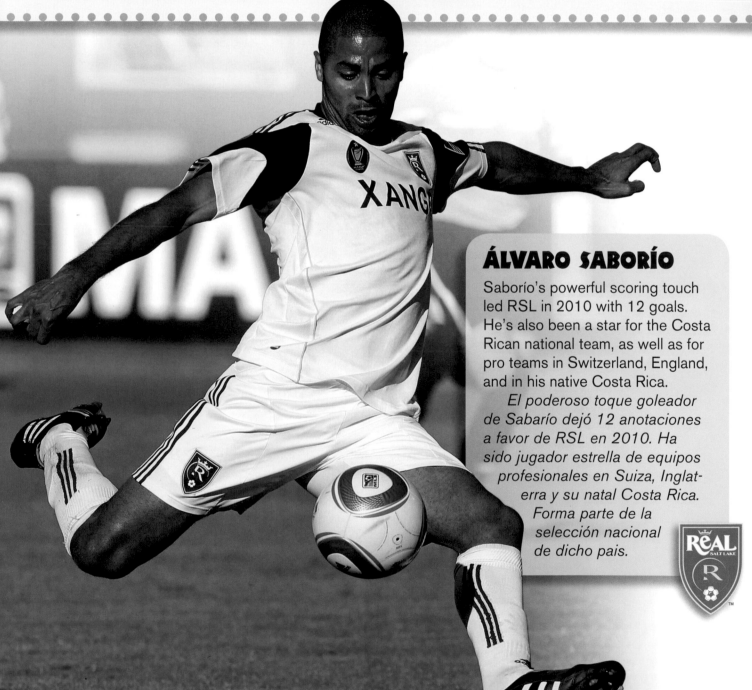

ÁLVARO SABORÍO

Saborío's powerful scoring touch led RSL in 2010 with 12 goals. He's also been a star for the Costa Rican national team, as well as for pro teams in Switzerland, England, and in his native Costa Rica.

El poderoso toque goleador de Sabarío dejó 12 anotaciones a favor de RSL en 2010. Ha sido jugador estrella de equipos profesionales en Suiza, Inglaterra y su natal Costa Rica. Forma parte de la selección nacional de dicho pais.

Have fun
with these
stickers!

STICKERS!

Find the team logos near all the players and put the right team stickers there.

Chicago Fire

D.C. United

Houston Dynamo

Philadelphia Union

Columbus Crew

New England Revolution

New York Red Bulls

Chivas USA

Toronto FC

FC Dallas

Colorado Rapids

San Jose Earthquakes

Portland Timbers

Vancouver Whitecaps FC

BONUS STICKER!
Major League Soccer

Los Angeles Galaxy

Argentina

Brazil

Canada

Colombia

Sporting
Kansas City

Costa Rica

England

Estonia

France

Seattle Sounders FC

Gambia

Ghana

Haiti

Jamaica

Japan

Mexico

Montenegro

Senegal

Real Salt Lake

Serbia

Sierra Leone

United States

BONUS STICKER!

JAMAICA

CAPITAL: Kingston

POPULATION: 2.8 million

LANGUAGE: English

WORLD CUP APPEARANCES: 1   **WORLD CUP TITLES:** 0

MLS PLAYERS 2011: 12

▶ Jamaica is an island nation located south of Cuba in the Caribbean Sea.

▶ The island was a British colony from 1655 until full independence in 1962.

▶ Thousands of tourists flock to Jamaican resorts in Montego Bay and Runaway Bay for water sports and beautiful beaches.

DONOVAN RICKETTS

Since joining the Galaxy in 2009, Ricketts has become one of the league's top goalies. He averaged less than a goal a game in 2010, helping L.A. win the Western Conference title. Before joining MLS, Donovan played in England. He has also represented his native land more than 70 times in international play.

DANE RICHARDS

With attacking skills and a great passing eye, Richards is a multi-talented threat. The former Clemson University star set a career high with five goals in 2010. He also plays for the Jamaica national team. He loves to listen to reggae (REG-ay), a type of music created in Jamaica.

COLOMBIA

DAVID FERREIRA

No one had a better 2010 MLS season than David Ferreira. He was named the MLS MVP after scoring eight goals and adding 13 assists. David led FC Dallas to its first MLS Cup berth.

Nadie pudo haber tenido una major temporada 2010 en la MLS como David Ferreira quien fue nombrado como el "jugador más valioso" despues de marcar ocho goles y 13 pases a gol. Ferreira llevó FC Dallas a su primera final de la Copa MLS.

FACTS ABOUT **COLOMBIA**

CAPITAL: Bogotá

POPULATION: 45.6 million

LANGUAGE: Spanish

WORLD CUP APPEARANCES: 4

WORLD CUP TITLES: 0

MLS PLAYERS 2011: 16

▶ Colombia has beaches on both the Atlantic and Pacific Oceans.

▶ Colombia produces great coffee and is home to most of the world's emeralds.

▶ Colombia is the second-largest Spanish-speaking nation in the world, after Mexico.

▶ Jungles and rainforests filled with rare and amazing animals cover the southern half of the country.

JUAN PABLO ANGEL

Ángel has been a scoring machine in MLS since he first joined the Red Bulls in 2007. Currently with the LA Galaxy, the former Premier League star has scored more MLS goals (58 through 2010) since 2007 than any other player.

Ángel ha sido una máquina imparable al marcar goles desde que se unió a los Red Bulls en 2007. El jugador, quien antes era una estrella de la Premier League, ha marcado más goles en MLS (58 a través de 2010) desde 2007 que cualquier otro jugador.

SOCCER IN COLOMBIA

Colombia's pro soccer leagues include more than 100 teams. Established in 1937, the Federación Colombiana de Fútbol holds annual championships at all levels. Colombian teams also play in tournaments among South American teams, such as Copa America.

Fútbol en Colombia: Las ligas profesionales de fútbol en Colombia incluyen más de 100 equipos. Establecida en 1937, la Federación Colombiana de Fútbol tiene campeonatos anuales en todos niveles. Los equipos Colombianos también juegan en torneos con equipos de Sudamérica, como Copa América.

FREDY MONTERO

Montero was twice the top scorer in the Colombian league. He kept it up after joining Sounders FC in 2009, finishing third in MLS with 12 goals and winning Newcomer of the Year 2009.

Montero fue dos veces el mejor goleador en la liga Colombiana. Siguió así después de unirse a Sounders FC en 2009, terminando tercero en MLS con 12 goles y ganar el premio de Revelación del Año 2009.

ARGENTINA

CAPITAL: Buenos Aires
POPULATION: 41.8 million
LANGUAGE: Spanish
WORLD CUP APPEARANCES: 15
WORLD CUP TITLES: 2
MLS PLAYERS 2011: 4

▶ Mt. Aconcagua (22,841 ft./6,962 m) is the highest point in the Southern Hemisphere.

▶ Tierra del Fuego is the southernmost point in the Americas.

▶ Some experts call former Argentina star Diego Maradona one of the best players ever.

PABLO MASTROENI

The Colorado Rapids captain and all-time leader in games played (in MLS) was born in Argentina, but plays for the U.S. national team.

El capitán de los Colorado Rapids y el líder de todos tiempos en partidos jugados (en MLS) nació en Argentina, pero ahora juega por el equipo nacional de los Estados Unidos.

JAVIER MORALES

An exciting midfield leader for RSL, Morales helped the team win the 2009 MLS Cup and was named to the MLS Best XI in 2010.

Un líder en la media cancha para RSL, Morales ayudó al equipo a ganar la MLS Cup 2009 y fue nombrado al Equipo Ideal de la MLS en 2010.

BRAZIL

CAPITAL: Brasilia

POPULATION: 184 million

LANGUAGE: Portuguese

WORLD CUP APPEARANCES: 19

WORLD CUP TITLES: 5

MLS PLAYERS 2011: 15

▶ Brazil is the largest country in South America.

▶ The Amazon River rainforest is almost as large as the continental U.S.

▶ Brazil's beaches draw millions of tourists as well as many beach soccer players.

▶ The largest city is Sao Paulo.

JUNINHO

Like many Brazilian players, Juninho goes by one name. Another name Galaxy fans will use for him is awesome! He has great midfield skills, but also a nose for the goal. One of his goals was runner-up for AT&T MLS Goal of the Year in 2010. Juninho started out in pro soccer in his hometown of Sao Paulo.

MAICON SANTOS

Toronto fans expect scoring punch from this talented forward. He has a lot of experience, having played in four countries before moving to MLS in 2009 with Chivas.

SOCCER IN **BRAZIL**

Since the beginning of the 20th century, soccer has been king in Brazil. The nation has a large pro soccer league with dozens of teams. Fans pack stadiums around the country, including the famous Maracana. Seating nearly 200,000 people, it's the largest in the world. Brazil's five World Cup titles are the most ever. Brazil will host the tournament in 2014.

ENGLAND

CAPITAL: London

POPULATION: 69.7 million (U.K.)

LANGUAGE: English

WORLD CUP APPEARANCES: 13

WORLD CUP TITLES: 1

MLS PLAYERS 2011: 12

▶ England is part of Great Britain, which also includes Scotland, Wales, and Northern Ireland.

▶ Parts of England were once controlled by the ancient Roman Empire.

▶ Queen Elizabeth II has reigned since 1952.

DAVID BECKHAM

"Becks" is one of the most famous and successful soccer players in the world. His amazing ability on free kicks and his smart midfield play has helped him play for England in three World Cups. He joined the Galaxy in 2007 after a great club career that included stints in England, Italy, and Spain.

ANDY IRO

Size and power have made Iro a top defender for the Crew. He is building on a career that started in college with All-America honors at UC Santa Barbara.

SOCCER IN ENGLAND

The birthplace of the sport, England is also home to dozens of pro teams. At the top is the Premier League, one of the most popular in the world, with devoted fans in many countries. England won its only World Cup in 1966.

FRANCE

CAPITAL: Paris

POPULATION: 65 million

LANGUAGE: French

WORLD CUP APPEARANCES: 13

WORLD CUP TITLES: 1

MLS PLAYERS 2011: 6

▶ France gets its name from the Franks, a people who lived there 2,000 years ago.

▶ France is one of the most famous winemaking regions in the world.

▶ Paris is one of the most popular places for Americans to visit.

THIERRY HENRY

Henry has been one of the most dangerous scoring threats in world soccer since he started playing in 1994. He was a star with English, Spanish, and Italian clubs for many years. He's France's all-time leading scorer. He scored three goals on the way to helping France win the 1998 World Cup.

SEBASTIEN LE TOUX

A big presence up front for the Union, Le Toux was named to the MLS Best XI in 2010 after scoring 14 goals and and getting 11 assists. How important was he to Philadelphia? The former Seattle star was part of more than 71 percent of their goals in 2010!

SERBIA

CAPITAL: Belgrade

POPULATION: 7.3 million

LANGUAGE: Serbian

WORLD CUP APPEARANCES: 11*

WORLD CUP TITLES: 0

MLS PLAYERS 2011: 7

*Includes appearances as Yugoslavia.

▶ Serbia is one of several countries formed by the breakup of Yugoslavia.

▶ Tourists enjoy visiting many of Serbia's ancient castles and forts.

▶ Hungry? Try Serbia's hamburger, called *pljeskavica* [PLEZ-kah-vee-sha].

MARKO PEROVIC

Midfielder Perovic was the MVP of the Revolution in 2010 after leading the team in goals. He boasts a powerful left foot and excels at free kicks. Before joining MLS, he was a star with a pro team in Switzerland, and he also played for many years in his native Belgrade.

ILIJA STOLICA

New England has a powerful pair of Serbians in Perovic and Stolica. Teaming up in 2010, the pair were part of nearly half of New England's goals. Stolica also played for clubs in Serbia before joining MLS. A strong force on the front line, he has also played in Greece and Belgium.

JAPAN

CAPITAL: Tokyo

POPULATION: 126.5 million

LANGUAGE: Japanese

WORLD CUP APPEARANCES: 4

WORLD CUP TITLES: 0

MLS PLAYERS 2011: 1

▶ Japan is a large island along with many smaller islands.

▶ To Japanese people, their country is known as Nippon.

▶ More cars are made in Japan than in any other country.

▶ In Japan, May 5 is Children's Day . . . cool!

KOSUKE KIMURA

In 2007, Kimura became the first player from Japan in MLS. In 2010, he scored the goal that sent the Rapids into the MLS Cup. He joined his teammates in winning the club's first MLS championship (right). A solid defender, he has the skills to get into the offense, too.

SOCCER IN JAPAN

Soccer has boomed in Japan in the past decade. The sport has been played there since the 1800s, but things have picked up lately. In 1993, the pro J-League was started. After a slow start, it began to draw good crowds and stars from other nations. The national team made its first World Cup in 1998, and has played in each one since. In 2002, Japan was the co-host (with Korea) of the World Cup, and that drew millions of fans to the games.

GAMBIA

CAPITAL: Banjul

POPULATION: 1.8 million

LANGUAGE: English

WORLD CUP APPEARANCES: 0

WORLD CUP TITLES: 0

MLS PLAYERS 2011: 5

▶ Gambia gained its independence from Great Britain in 1965.

▶ The country is located on both banks of the long Gambia River in western Africa.

▶ The largest tribe is Mandinka.

▶ One of the biggest exports is peanuts.

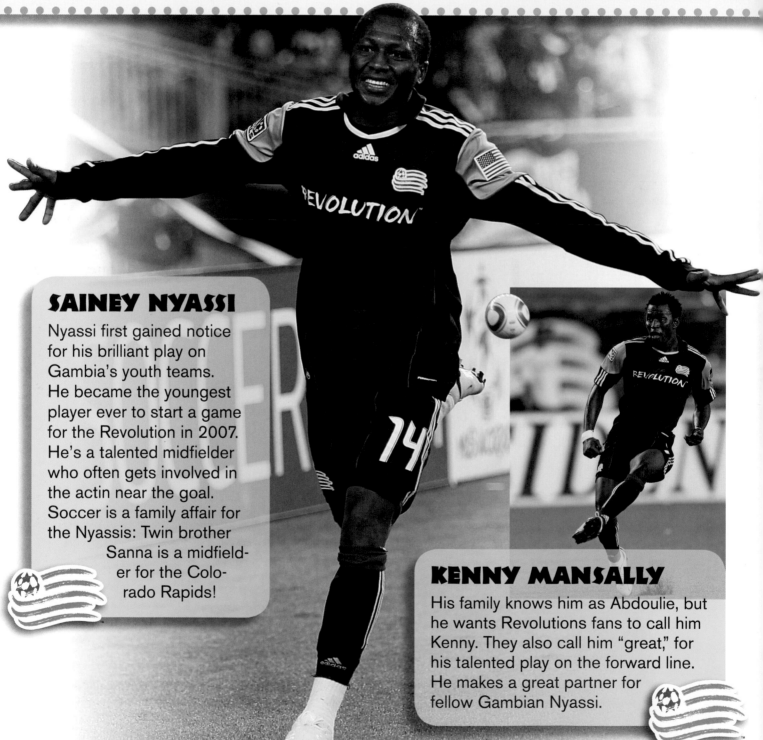

SAINEY NYASSI

Nyassi first gained notice for his brilliant play on Gambia's youth teams. He became the youngest player ever to start a game for the Revolution in 2007. He's a talented midfielder who often gets involved in the actin near the goal. Soccer is a family affair for the Nyassis: Twin brother Sanna is a midfielder for the Colorado Rapids!

KENNY MANSALLY

His family knows him as Abdoulie, but he wants Revolutions fans to call him Kenny. They also call him "great," for his talented play on the forward line. He makes a great partner for fellow Gambian Nyassi.

GHANA

CAPITAL: Accra

POPULATION: 24.8 million

LANGUAGE: English and others

WORLD CUP APPEARANCES: 2

WORLD CUP TITLES: 0

MLS PLAYERS 2011: 7

▶ Ghana became independent from Great Britain in 1957.

▶ Lake Volta and the Volta River form the backbone of Ghana.

▶ Tourists visit the Kumasi area to see traditional African crafts and buildings.

▶ Ghana is a major gold-mining country.

ROBBIE RUSSELL

Russell's been a solid pro defender for a dozen years. His soccer travels have taken him to Iceland, Norway, and Denmark. But his greatest moment came in 2009. Russell's penalty-kick goal in a shootout was the clincher that gave RSL its first MLS Cup championship.

PATRICK NYARKO

After an All-America career at Virginia Tech, Nyarko became a regular starter on the wing for the Fire in 2009. There he's able to use his tremendous speed and nose for the goal in the attack. He's super-dependable, too. Nyarko played the most games of any Fire player in 2009 and 2010.

SENEGAL BOUNA COUNDOUL

In 2010, Coundoul set a Red Bulls record with 11 shutouts as the team had one of the best defenses in the league. Quick and athletic, he's emerging as one of the best MLS keepers. Bouna has also won several awards for his community work.

CAPITAL: Dakar   **POPULATION:** 12.6 million

LANGUAGE: French   **WORLD CUP APPEARANCES:** 1

WORLD CUP TITLES: 0   **MLS PLAYERS 2011:** 3

▶ A Senegal national park called Djoudj is one of the world's best places for birdwatching.

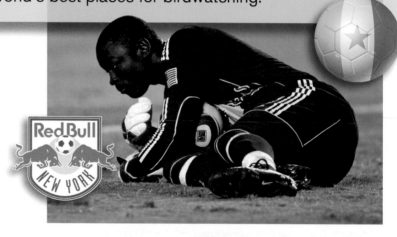

MONTENEGRO
BRANKO BOSKOVIC

Boskovic proudly played in the first international game ever for Montenegro, which joined the world soccer community in 2007. He joined United in 2010 after playing for clubs in Austria, France, and Serbia.

CAPITAL: Podgorica

POPULATION: .6 million

LANGUAGE: Montenegrin

WORLD CUP APPEARANCES: 0

WORLD CUP TITLES: 0

MLS PLAYERS 2011: 1

▶ One of the world's newest countries, Montenegro declared its independence in 2006.

HAITI
JAMES MARCELIN

Marcelin brings international experience to his role as a midfielder on one of the new MLS teams for 2011. Before joining Portland, he played professionally in Puerto Rico, and has played for Haiti since 2007.

CAPITAL: Port-au-Prince

POPULATION: 2.8 million

LANGUAGE: English

WORLD CUP APPEARANCES: 1

WORLD CUP TITLES: 0

MLS PLAYERS ALL-TIME: 2

▶ Haiti is western half of an island in the Caribbean Sea.

ESTONIA JOEL LINDPERE

This veteran midfielder continues to outwork and outhustle younger players. The Red Bull MVP in 2010 while leading the team in assists, he has also played more than 70 matches for his national team.

CAPITAL: Tallinn

POPULATION: 1.3 million

LANGUAGE: Estonian

WORLD CUP APPEARANCES: 0

WORLD CUP TITLES: 0

MLS PLAYERS 2011: 1

▶ Independent again since 1994, Estonia is one of the three "Baltic" nations.

SIERRA LEONE
KEI KAMARA

In his fifth MLS season in 2010, Kamara blossomed into a star. He was Kansas City's leading scorer with 10 goals and was named the team's MVP. His height and goal sense make him a very dangerous striker.

CAPITAL: Freetown

POPULATION: 5.4 million

LANGUAGE: English

WORLD CUP APPEARANCES: 1

WORLD CUP TITLES: 0

MLS PLAYERS 2011: 2

▶ Once a British colony, this country's name means "Lion Mountains."

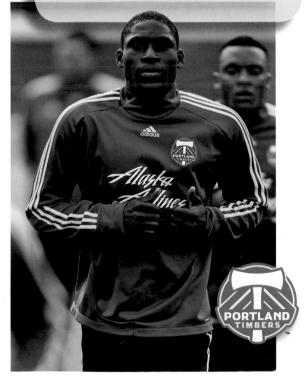

Tracking Thierry!

Thierry Henry has to find his way to the goal. Follow the twisting paths and pick out the one that will help him score!

Scoreboard Trouble!

A computer virus has caused problems at the soccer scoreboard. These important soccer words are all mixed up! Can you unscramble the words? Then use the letters in the circles to discover what countries around the world call soccer.

1. __ ◯ __ __ **LGAO** A score in soccer

2. __ __ __ __ __ ◯ **SITSAS** A pass that leads to a score

3. __ __ __ __ __ __ __ __ __ __ **RCENOR CKKI** The restart after the defense kicks the ball over the end line

4. __ ◯ __ __ __ __ **KTLECA** When a player takes the ball away from a dribbler

5. __ __ __ __ ◯ __ __ **OWTRH NI** Restart after the ball goes over the sidelines

6. __ __ __ __ __ __ **IFKOKCF** How each game begins

7. __ __ __ ◯ __ __ __ **BRIBDEL** To move the ball with your feet using short taps

8. __ ◯ ◯ __ __ __ __ **OWLDR UPC** Soccer's international championship

Secret Word: F __ __ __ __ __ __ __

MLS Word Search!

Find these words from MLS team names listed below in this soccer-ball shaped word grid. Just like the ball moves in every direction on a soccer field, the words in this grid can be found up, down, diagonally . . . or even backward!

Chivas USA
Crew
Dynamo
Earthquakes
FC Dallas
Fire
Galaxy
Rapids
Real
Red Bulls
Revolution
Sporting
Sounders
Timbers
Toronto FC
Union
United
Whitecaps

Puzzle Answers

MLS Word Search

MLS COUNTRIES

Here are all the nations in which MLS players were born.
The list is as of the beginning of the 2011 season.
The countries in red are featured in this book.

Argentina	Denmark	Ivory Coast	Serbia
Belgium	Ecuador	Jamaica	Sierra Leone
Bosnia & Herzegovina	England	Japan	South Africa
Brazil	Finland	Liberia	St. Kitts & Nevis
Cameroon	Estonia	Mexico	Sweden
Canada	France	Montenegro	Switzerland
Chile	Gambia	Morocco	Tanzania
China	Georgia	Netherlands	Trinidad & Tobago
Colombia	Ghana	New Zealand	Uganda
Costa Rica	Grenada	Nigeria	Uruguay
Croatia	Guadeloupe	Norway	United States
Cuba	Guatemala	Peru	Venezuela
Curaçao	Haiti	Poland	Wales
Democratic Republic of the Congo	Honduras	Scotland	Zimbabwe
	Israel	Senegal	

MLS W.O.R.K.S.™

MLS W.O.R.K.S. Active Bodies Active Minds (ABAM) program is a soccer-centered community outreach initiative that provides resources to motivate and reward children for being mentally and physically fit.

Join the **Active Bodies Active Minds Club** and receive access to fitness, nutrition and reading resources to help you stay active during the summer and year round. Sign up today and become eligible for ABAM Sweepstakes that could send you and your family to the 2011 AT&T MLS All-Star game or MLS Cup 2011!

Plus, qualify to win autographed merchandise from some of your favorite Major League Soccer clubs and players!

Sign up today at **www.JoinABAM.com**

Active Bodies Active Minds reading and fitness program gives you more fun ways to keep young brains and bodies moving and growing!
Learn more at
www.joinabam.com.

MLS W.O.R.K.S., Major League Soccer's community outreach initiative, is dedicated to addressing important issues affecting young people and serves as a platform for both League and club philanthropic programs. MLS W.O.R.K.S. has joined in the fight against childhood obesity and seeks to encourage children throughout North America to live a healthy, active lifestyle.